| BN | WH | WY | CH |
|---|---|---|---|
| 2/19 | 1/20 | 12/21 | 5/24 |

BENSON LIBRARY
CASTLE SQUARE
BENSON OX10 6SD
TEL. 01491 838474

Chinnor Library
Station Road
Chinnor
Oxon OX39 4PU
Tel (01844) 351721

WHEATLEY LIBRARY
THE MERRY BELLS
HIGH STREET
WHEATLEY
OXFORD OX33 1XP
Tel: 01865 875267

WYCHWOOD LIBRARY
29 HIGH ST,
MILTON UNDER WYCHWOOD
OXFORD OX7 6LD
TEL: 01993 830281

To renew this book, phone 0845 1202811 or visit
our website at www.libcat.oxfordshire.gov.uk
You will need your library PIN number
(available from your library)

**OXFORDSHIRE COUNTY COUNCIL**
Social & Community Services
www.oxfordshire.gov.uk

3303460572

**BRIGHT IDEA BOOKS**

# HOW DO Snakes POO?

Malta Cunningham

raintree
a Capstone company — publishers for children

Raintree is an imprint of Capstone Global Library Limited, a company incorporated in England and Wales having its registered office at 264 Banbury Road, Oxford, OX2 7DY – Registered company number: 6695582

www.raintree.co.uk
myorders@raintree.co.uk

Text © Capstone Global Library Limited 2019
The moral rights of the proprietor have been asserted.

All rights reserved. No part of this publication may be reproduced in any form or by any means (including photocopying or storing it in any medium by electronic means and whether or not transiently or incidentally to some other use of this publication) without the written permission of the copyright owner, except in accordance with the provisions of the Copyright, Designs and Patents Act 1988 or under the terms of a licence issued by the Copyright Licensing Agency, Barnard's Inn, 86 Fetter Lane, London, EC4A 1EN (www.cla.co.uk). Applications for the copyright owner's written permission should be addressed to the publisher.

Edited by Maddie Spalding
Designed by Becky Daum
Production by Laura Polzin
Printed and bound in India

ISBN 978 1 4747 7511 3
22 21 20 19 18
10 9 8 7 6 5 4 3 2 1

**British Library Cataloguing in Publication Data**
A full catalogue record for this book is available from the British Library.

**Acknowledgements**
iStockphoto: danlogan, 13, ilbusca, 31, JedsPics_com, 8–9, Mark Kostich, 16–17, MelanieMaya, 10–11; Science Source: Hugh Lansdown/FLPA/Science Source, 14–15; Shutterstock Images: beejung, 26–27, feathercollector, 21, fototrips, cover (snake), harmpeti, 18–19, 29, Heiko Kiera, 24–25, Kaliva, 22–23, Matt Jeppson, 5, phichak, cover (poo), reptiles4all, 7, Zhukov Oleg, cover (background)
Design Elements: iStockphoto, Red Line Editorial, and Shutterstock Images

We would like to thank Charles Smith, PhD, Associate Professor of Biology, Wofford College for his invaluable help in the preparation of this book.

Every effort has been made to contact copyright holders of material reproduced in this book. Any omissions will be rectified in subsequent printings if notice is given to the publisher.

All the internet addresses (URLs) given in this book were valid at the time of going to press. However, due to the dynamic nature of the internet, some addresses may have changed, or sites may have changed or ceased to exist since publication. While the author and publisher regret any inconvenience this may cause readers, no responsibility for any such changes can be accepted by either the author or the publisher.

# CONTENTS

**CHAPTER 1**
**SNAKE SURPRISE!** ............ 4

**CHAPTER 2**
**GETTING FOOD** ................ 6

**CHAPTER 3**
**SNAKE POO** .................... 12

**CHAPTER 4**
**STRANGE SNAKES** ............ 20

Glossary ............................. 28
Top five reasons why
snakes are awesome ........... 29
Activity ............................... 30
Find out more ..................... 32
Index .................................. 32

# CHAPTER 1

# SNAKE Surprise!

A hiker walks down a path. The sun is bright in the sky. The hiker wipes sweat off his forehead. He looks around.

He finds a rock to sit on. The rock has a dark smudge. He leans in closer. Hairs and bones are poking out. The hiker recognizes the smudge. It's snake poo!

**Snakes often warm themselves on hot rocks.**

CHAPTER 2

# GETTING Food

A snake needs to eat before it can poo. Snakes find food in many ways. Some wait for **prey** to come to them. Others hunt for prey.

A snake uses its tongue to find prey. Prey give off chemicals. The snake's tongue picks up the chemicals. Then the snake can find the prey. The snake opens its mouth wide. It grabs its prey.

A snake flicks its tongue out of its mouth to help it find prey.

Snakes open their jaws wide to eat prey. Some can even eat deer!

8

Some snakes kill with **venom**. The venom comes from their **fangs**. These snakes bite their prey.

Other snakes swallow live prey. A snake's jaws are connected with tissue. The tissue is **flexible**. It allows the snake's jaws to open wide.

## JACOBSON'S ORGAN

A snake's tongue carries chemicals to a special organ. The organ is in the roof of its mouth. This organ can identify the chemicals.

Some snakes wrap their bodies around their prey. They squeeze hard. This cuts off the prey's blood supply. Its heart can't pump blood. Then the prey dies. The snake swallows it whole!

## A LARGE MEAL

In Australia, a python killed and ate a crocodile. The python was 3.1 metres (10 feet) long. The crocodile was 0.9 metres (3 feet) long.

Squeezing prey also stops it from escaping.

11

# CHAPTER 3

# SNAKE Poo

Prey is a snake's food. A snake needs to **digest** what it eats. Food enters the stomach. The stomach is shaped like a tube. Juices break down food. The food moves through the snake's **intestines**. It comes out as poo.

Some snakes that live in or near water eat fish.

Snake poo comes in all shapes and sizes!

14

Snake poo comes out of a hole. The hole is on the bottom of the snake's body. Sometimes the poo is brown. Other times it has white in it. Usually the poo is wet.

## URIC ACID

A snake's digestive system breaks down proteins. This produces uric acid. This is the white part of a snake's poo.

Many snakes eat mice or rats. Bush vipers hunt prey from trees.

Often there are fur and bones in a snake's poo. These are from animals the snake ate. Some snakes eat mice or frogs. Some eat other snakes. Then they have scales in their poo!

## HOLD IT IN!

Snakes do not eat often. They can go months without eating. This means they may not poo for months. Some pythons go more than a year without pooing. Gaboon vipers won't poo until they have to. One Gaboon viper went 420 days without pooing!

Gaboon vipers live in rainforests south of the Sahara Desert in Africa.

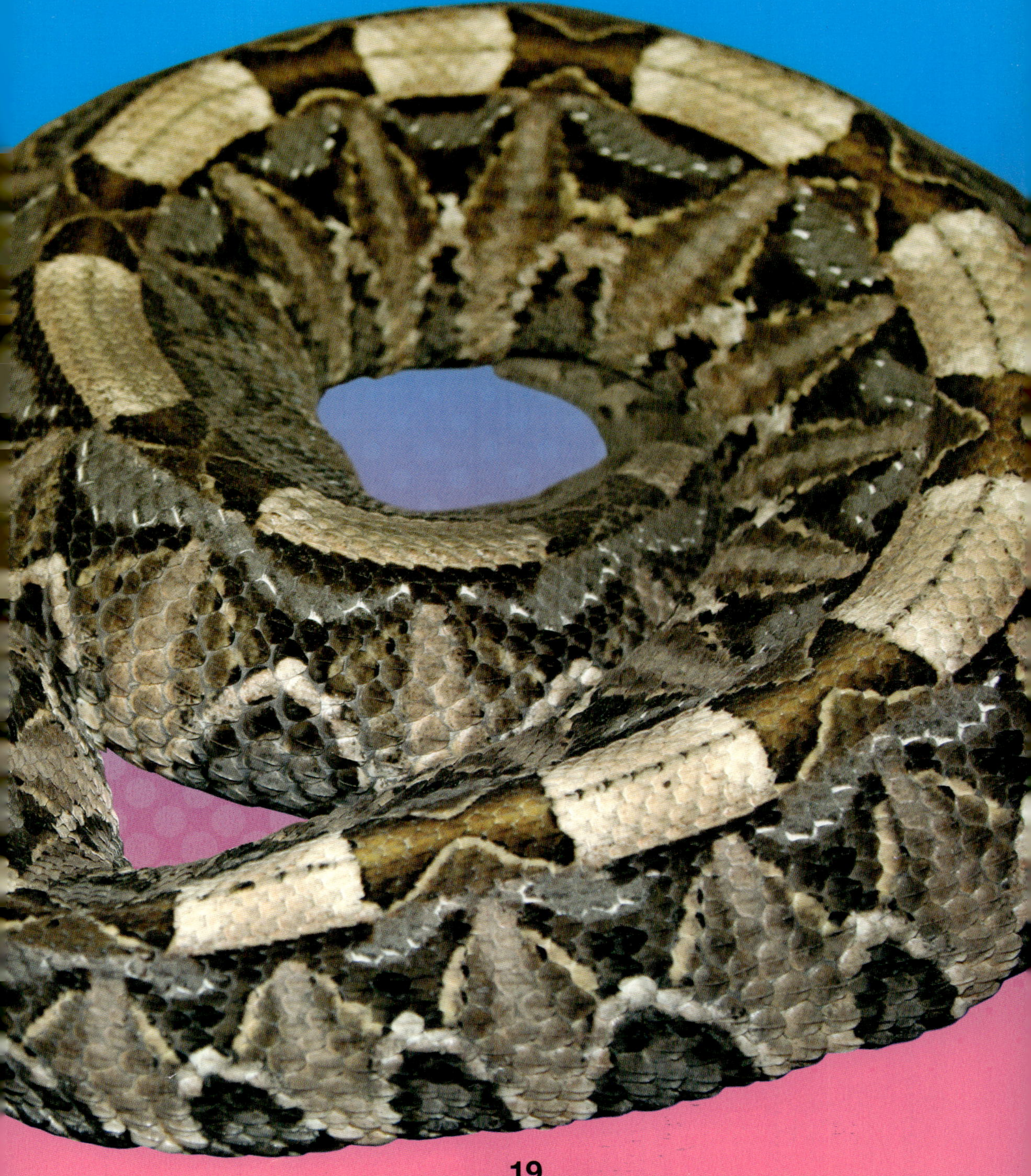

CHAPTER 4

# STRANGE Snakes

Snakes don't usually eat certain toads. Some toads have poison **glands** in their skin. But one type of snake in Japan eats poisonous toads. This snake is called the tiger keelback. It can't make poison.

But it steals poison from the toads it eats. It uses the poison to protect itself. It stores the poison in glands. The glands are on the back of its neck. The snake's **predators** bite or claw its neck. This rips the skin above the glands. The predator gets a mouthful of poison!

The tiger keelback snake sneaks up on prey. It bites toads before they can hop away.

## WHAT'S FOR LUNCH?

Some snakes are born with two heads. These snakes are rare. They often die in the wild. That's because both heads try to make decisions for one body. Both heads need to agree when they are hungry. They need to agree on what to eat. The two heads may fight over food. One head might try to eat the other!

**Two-headed snakes may share the same stomach and digestive organs.**

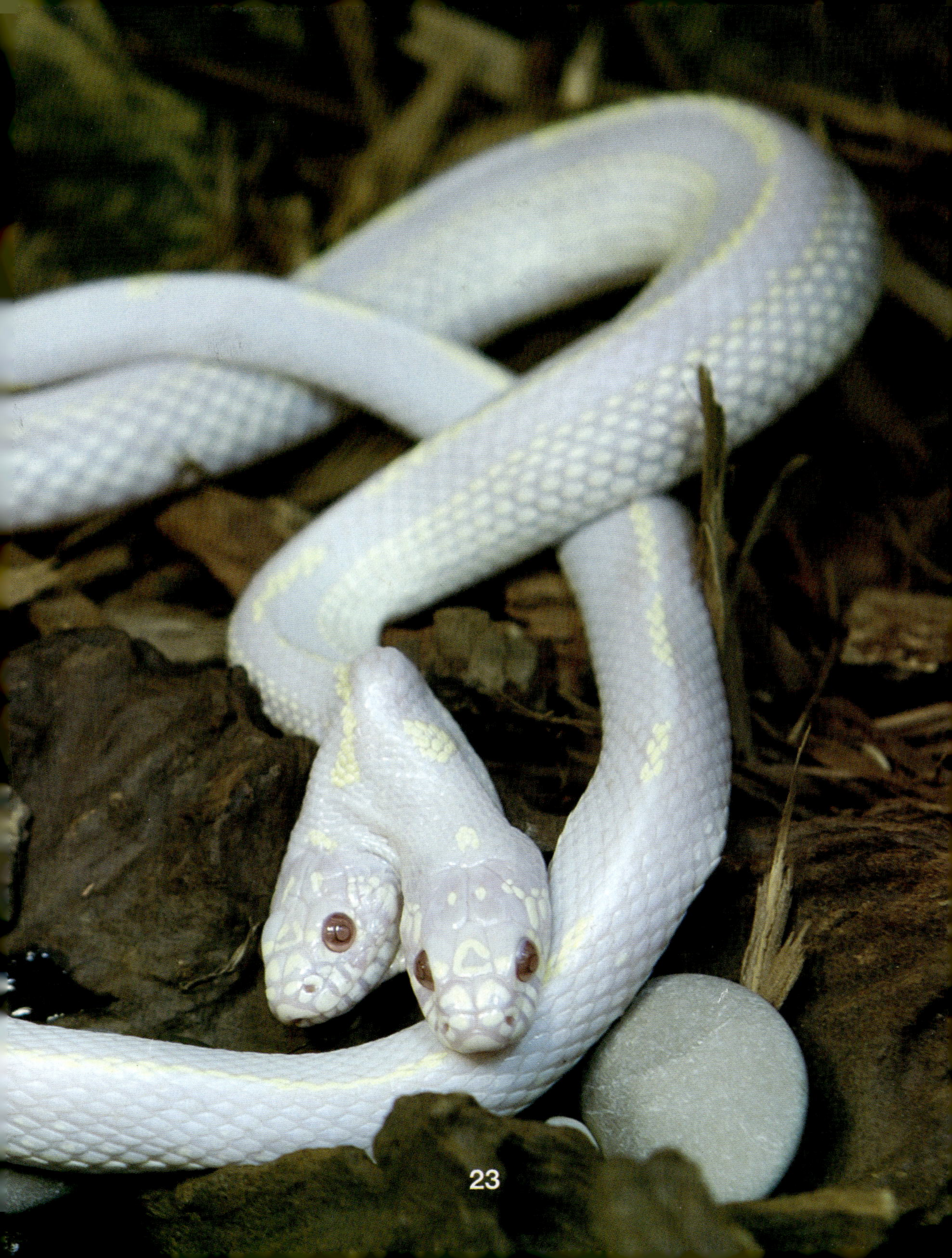

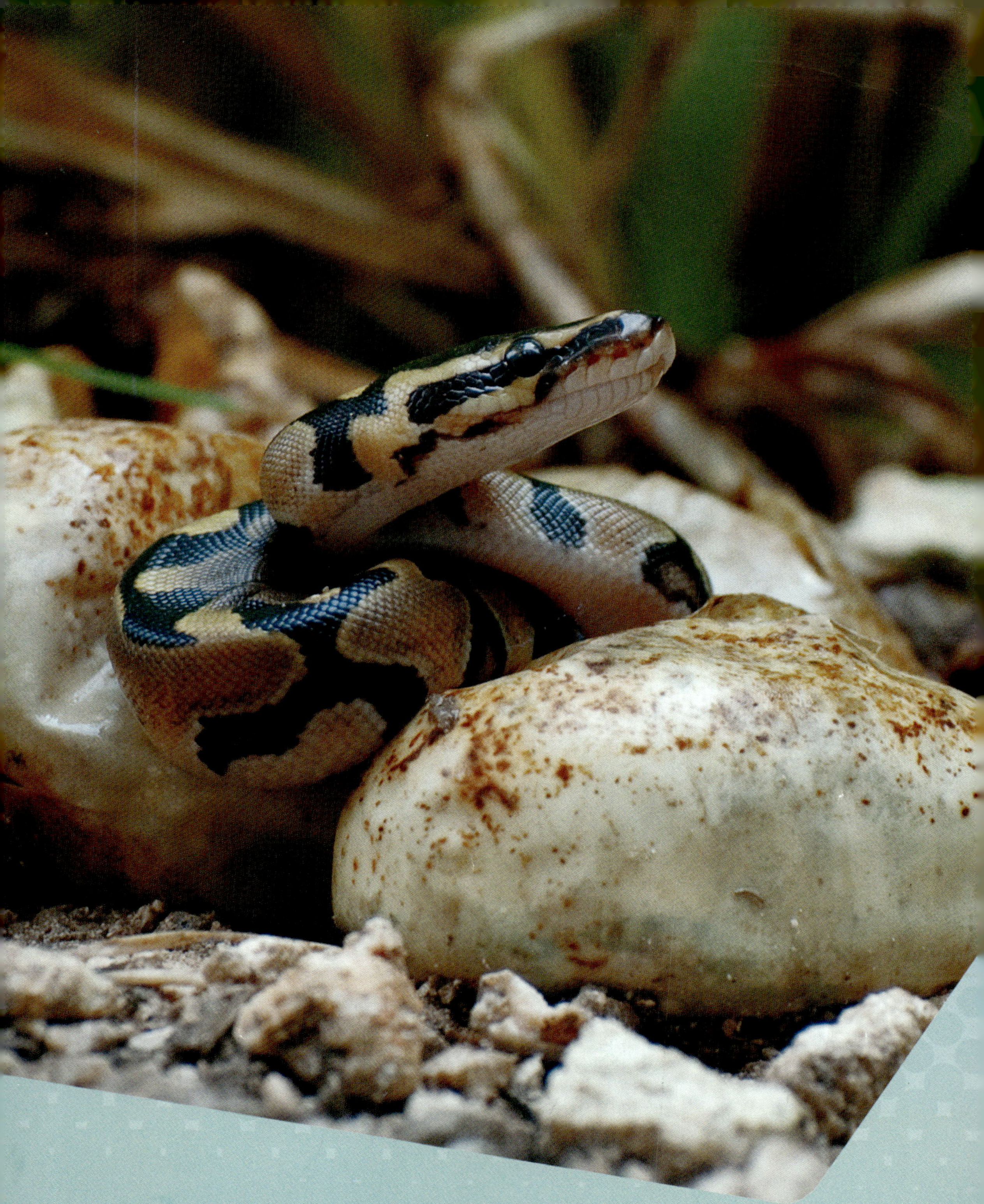

## SNAKES THAT EAT THEIR OFFSPRING

Female snakes may give birth to many offspring. Some snakes give birth to up to 80 offspring! Their offspring are called snakelets. Some snakelets do not survive.

Most snakes lay eggs. Snakelets hatch from the eggs.

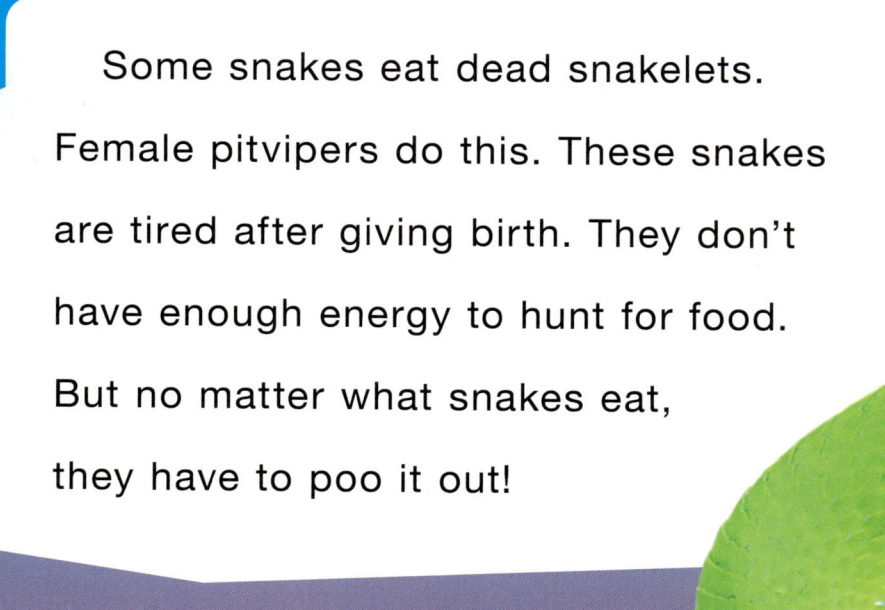

Some snakes eat dead snakelets. Female pitvipers do this. These snakes are tired after giving birth. They don't have enough energy to hunt for food. But no matter what snakes eat, they have to poo it out!

Some pitvipers live in trees.

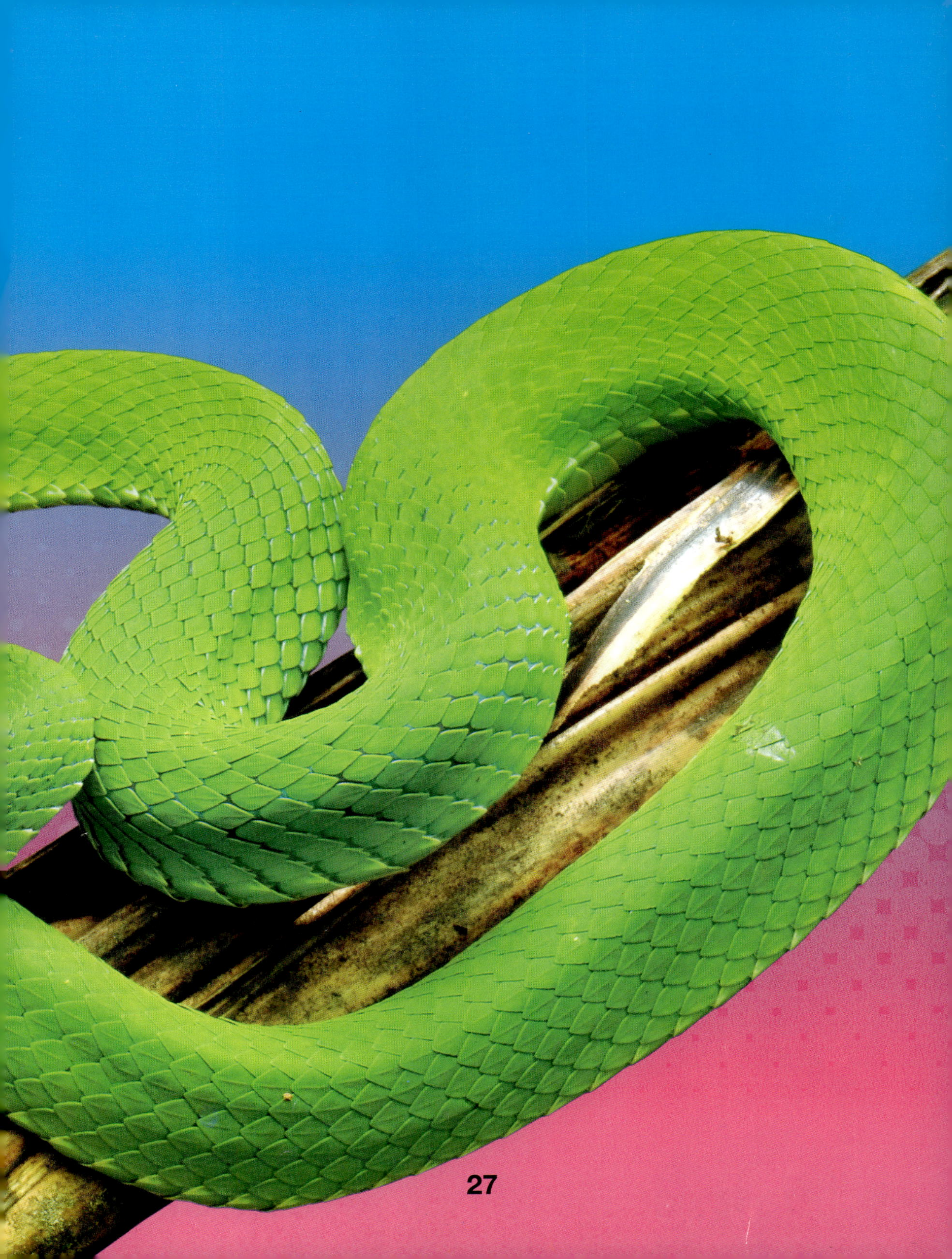

# GLOSSARY

**digest**
to break down food so the body can use it

**fang**
a long and sharp tooth that is hollow

**flexible**
able to move easily

**gland**
an organ that produces a certain substance in the body

**intestine**
an organ below the stomach that helps digest food

**predator**
an animal that kills and eats other animals

**prey**
an animal that is hunted by other animals for food

**venom**
liquid produced by some snakes that can kill prey

# TOP FIVE REASONS WHY SNAKES ARE AWESOME

1. Snakes can swallow prey alive.

2. Snakes can go for months without eating.

3. Some snakes may not poo for more than a year.

4. Some snakes can eat poisonous toads or newts.

5. Snakes live on every continent except Antarctica.

# ACTIVITY

Snake digestion is a bit different from human digestion. To discover how, try out this simple experiment:

**WHAT YOU WILL NEED**

1 sealable plastic bag
2 cheese crackers
1 can or bottle of fizzy drink

**INSTRUCTIONS**

1. Put the crackers in the plastic bag. Seal the bag shut. Squeeze and crush the crackers.

2. Open the bag. Pour in a small amount of fizzy drink. Seal the bag. Wait a few minutes and watch what happens.

The fizzy drink has acid. Your stomach also has acid. Acid breaks down your food. Your teeth start to break down your food first. Then it enters your stomach. Crushing the crackers is similar to chewing food. But snakes do not chew their food. They swallow it whole. Snakes digest their food at a slower rate than humans do. Why do you think this is? What might food look like in a snake's stomach?

HEART

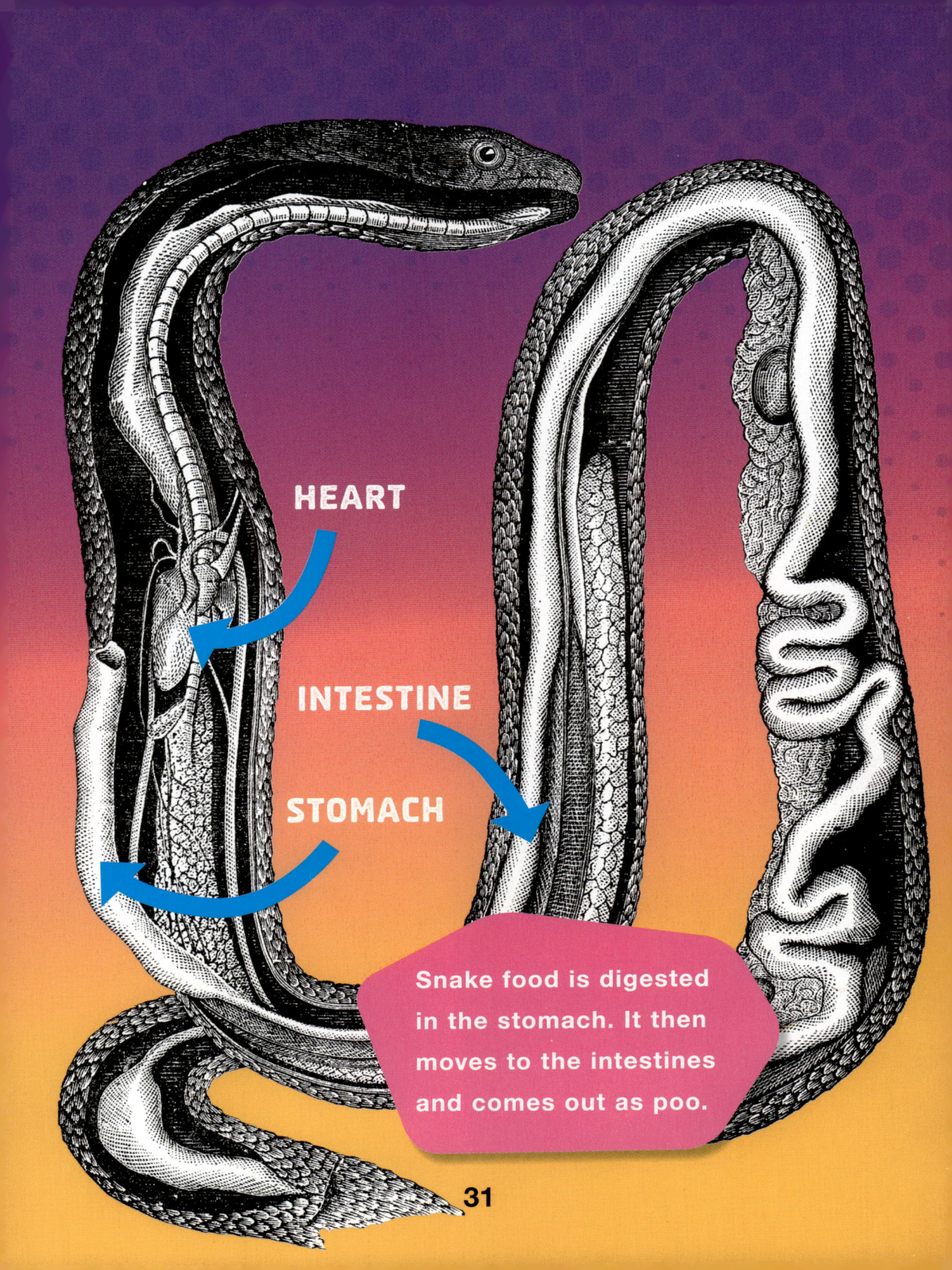

INTESTINE

STOMACH

Snake food is digested in the stomach. It then moves to the intestines and comes out as poo.

# FIND OUT MORE

Ready to discover more fun facts about snakes? Learn more with these resources.

## Books

*Everything You Need to Know About Snakes: And Other Scaly Reptiles*, John Woodward (DK, 2013)

*Snakes* (Built for the Hunt), Tammy Gagne (Raintree, 2016)

*Snakes* (Usborne Beginners), James MacLaine (Usborne, 2014)

## Websites

National Geographic: Rattlesnake
kids.nationalgeographic.com/animals/rattlesnake/

National Geographic: Super Snakes
kids.nationalgeographic.com/explore/nature/super-snakes/

# INDEX

digestion 12, 15
fangs 9
Gaboon viper 18
hunting 6–7, 26
Jacobson's organ 9
jaws 9
pitvipers 26
poo 5, 6, 12, 15, 17, 18, 26
predators 21
prey 6–7, 9–10, 12, 17, 20
pythons 10, 18
snakelets 25–26
tiger keelback snakes 20–21
two-headed snakes 22
venom 9